JAMAICA BAY FIELD TRIPS

JAMAICA BAY PAMPHLET LIBRARY 10

JAMAICA BAY FIELD TRIPS

STRUCTURES OF COASTAL RESILIENCE

Jamaica Bay Team
Spitzer School of Architecture
The City College of New York

Catherine Seavitt Nordenson, editor
Associate Professor of Landscape Architecture

Kjirsten Alexander
Research Associate

Danae Alessi
Research Associate

Eli Sands
Research Assistant

JAMAICA BAY PAMPHLET LIBRARY
10 Jamaica Bay Field Trips

ISBN 978-1-942900-10-8

COPYRIGHT

CONTACT

Catherine Seavitt Nordenson
cseavittnordenson@ccny.cuny.edu
www.structuresofcoastalresilience.org

SCR Jamaica Bay Team
The City College of New York
Spitzer School of Architecture
Program in Landscape Architecture, Room 2M24A
141 Convent Avenue New York, New York 10031

COVER

Machinery at Plumb Beach.
photo: Kjirsten Alexander

supported by

Rulers Bar community marsh planting, 2014

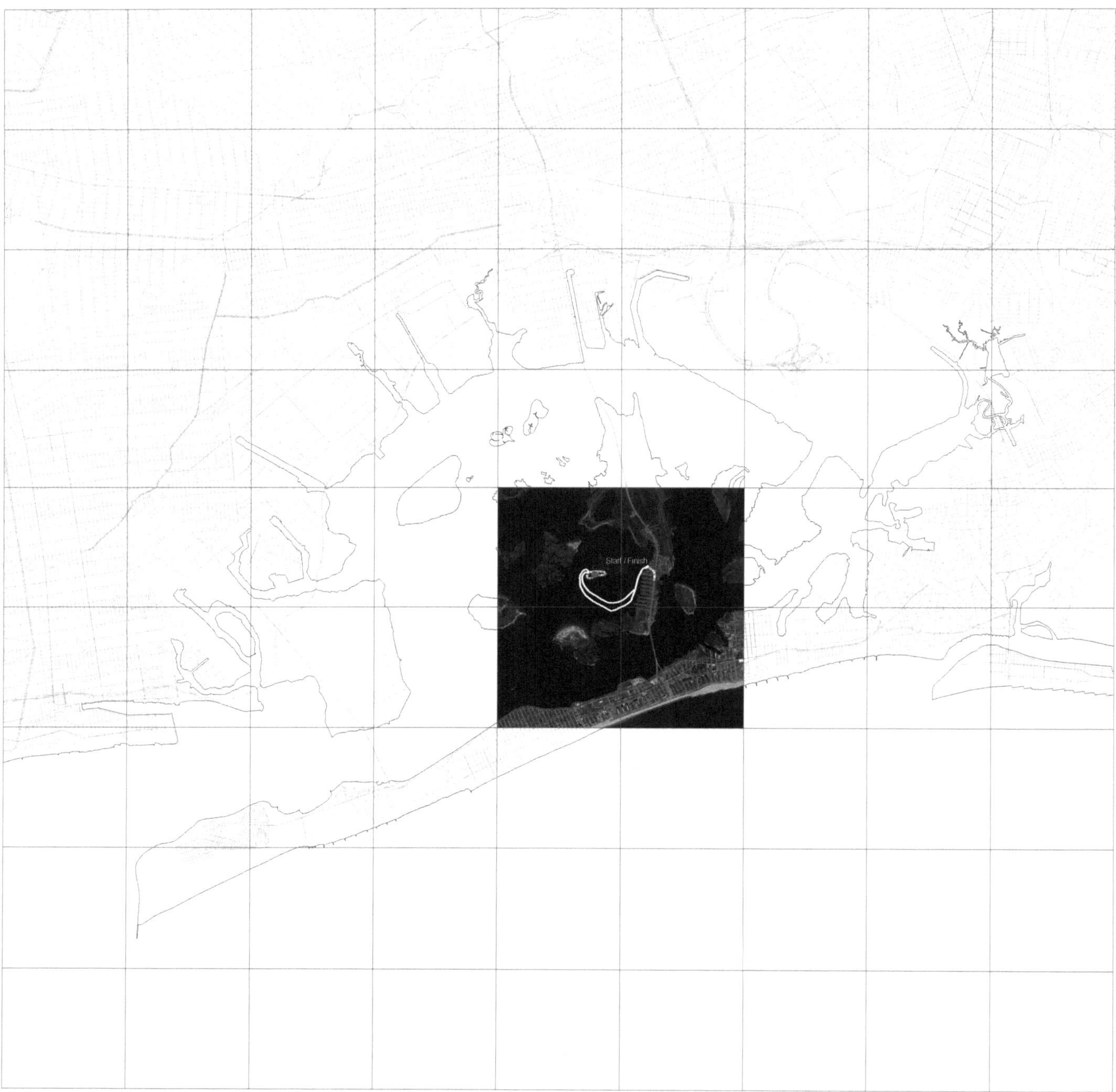

Black Wall Community Marsh Planting

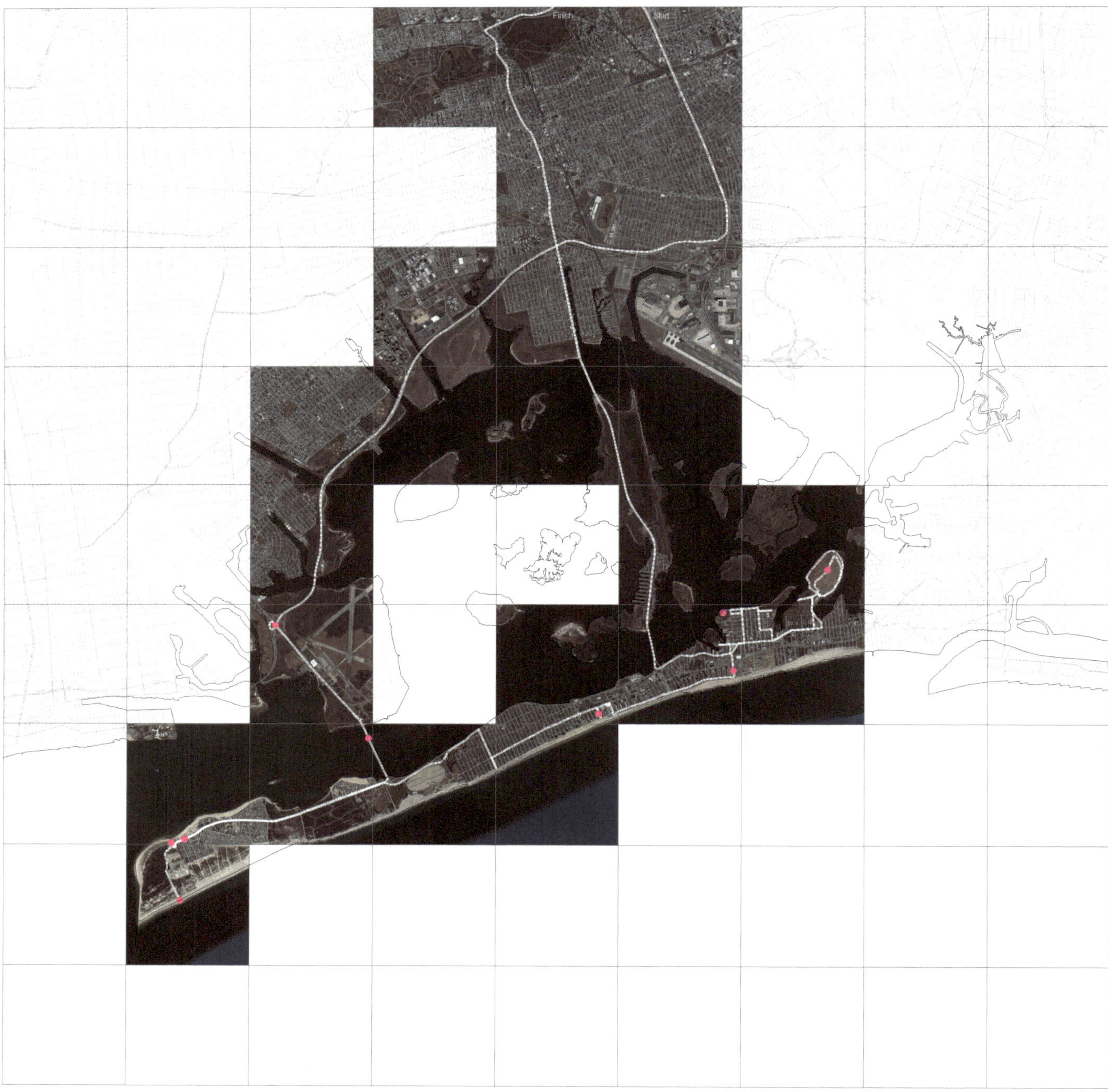

Belt Parkway, Breezy Point, Rockaway Survey

Rockaway Beach
Start
AREA
CLOSED
DO NOT ENTER
Finish

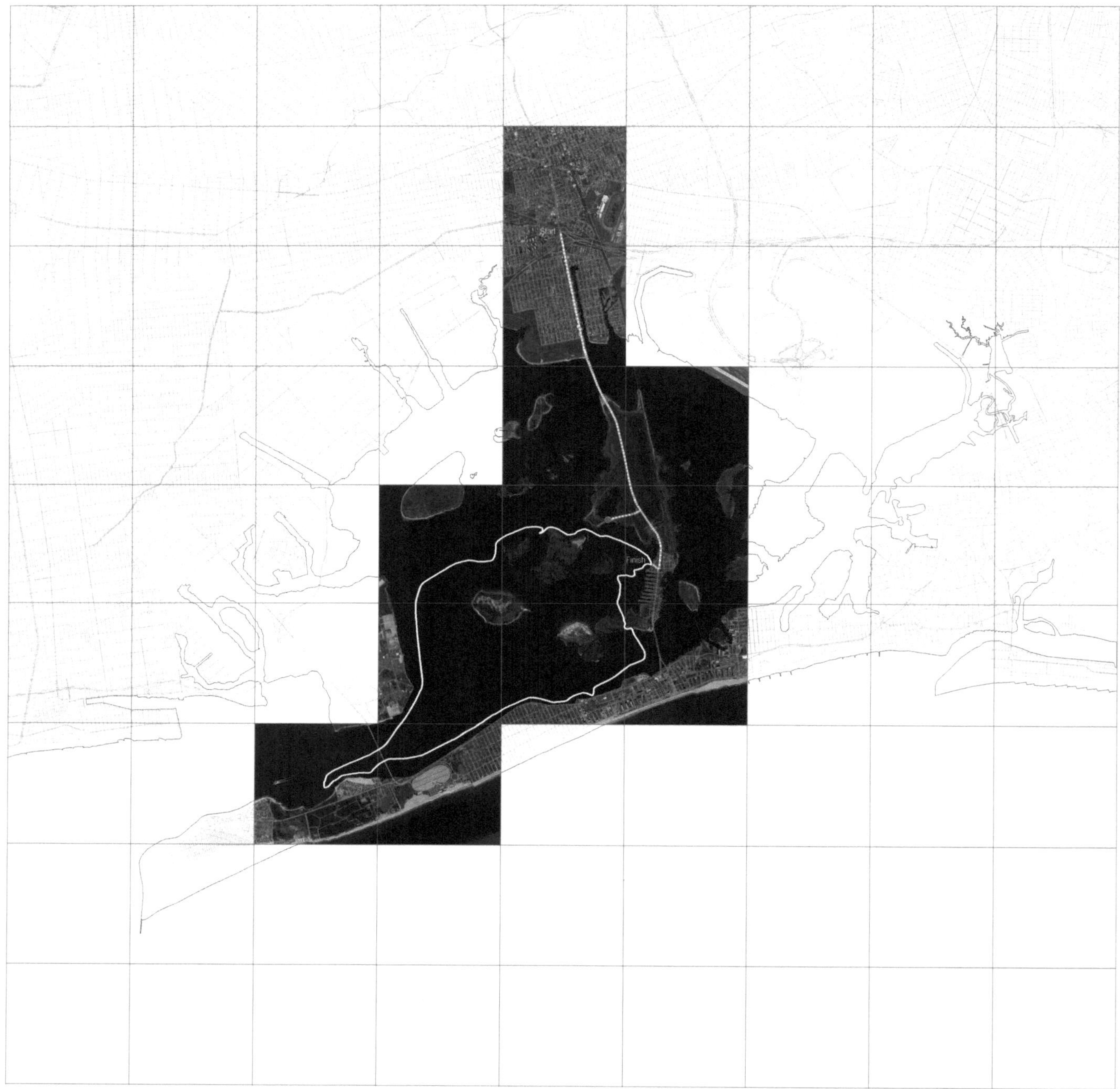

Yellow Bar Hassock, Stony Creek Marsh, Rockaway Inlet, Big Egg Marsh Boat Survey

TRAIL
CLOSED

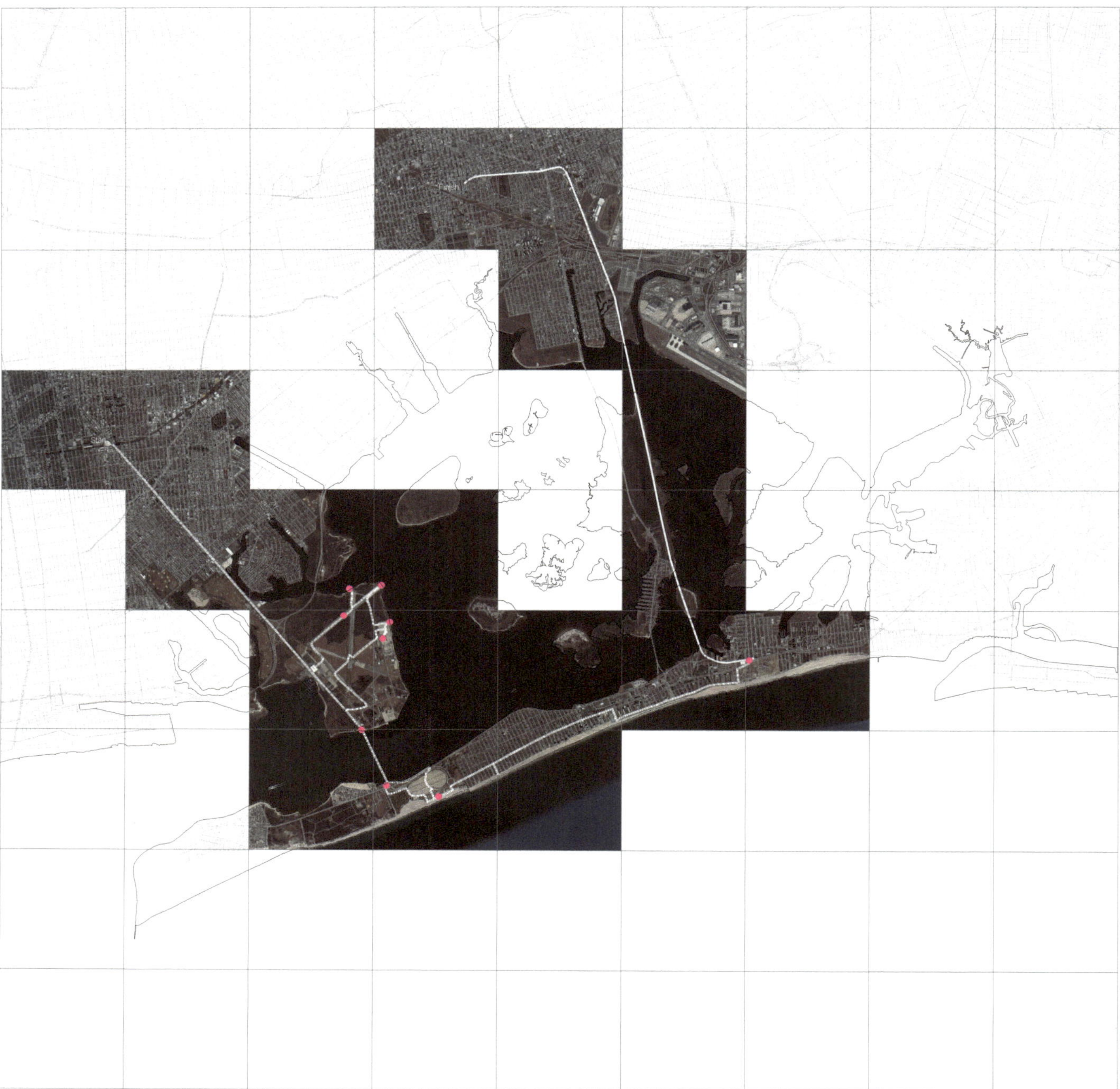

Floyd Bennett Field, Jacob Riis Park Bike Survey

Start
SPEED
LIMIT
ROAD
CLOSED
No parking in striped area
AREA
CLOSED
ALL NATIONAL PARK SERVICE AREA
BEYOND THIS POINT CLOSED TO
PUBLIC USE AND TRAVEL BECAUSE
OF EMERGENCY CONDITIONS
106
Finish

Jamaica Bay Wildlife Refuge Survey

Start
Finish

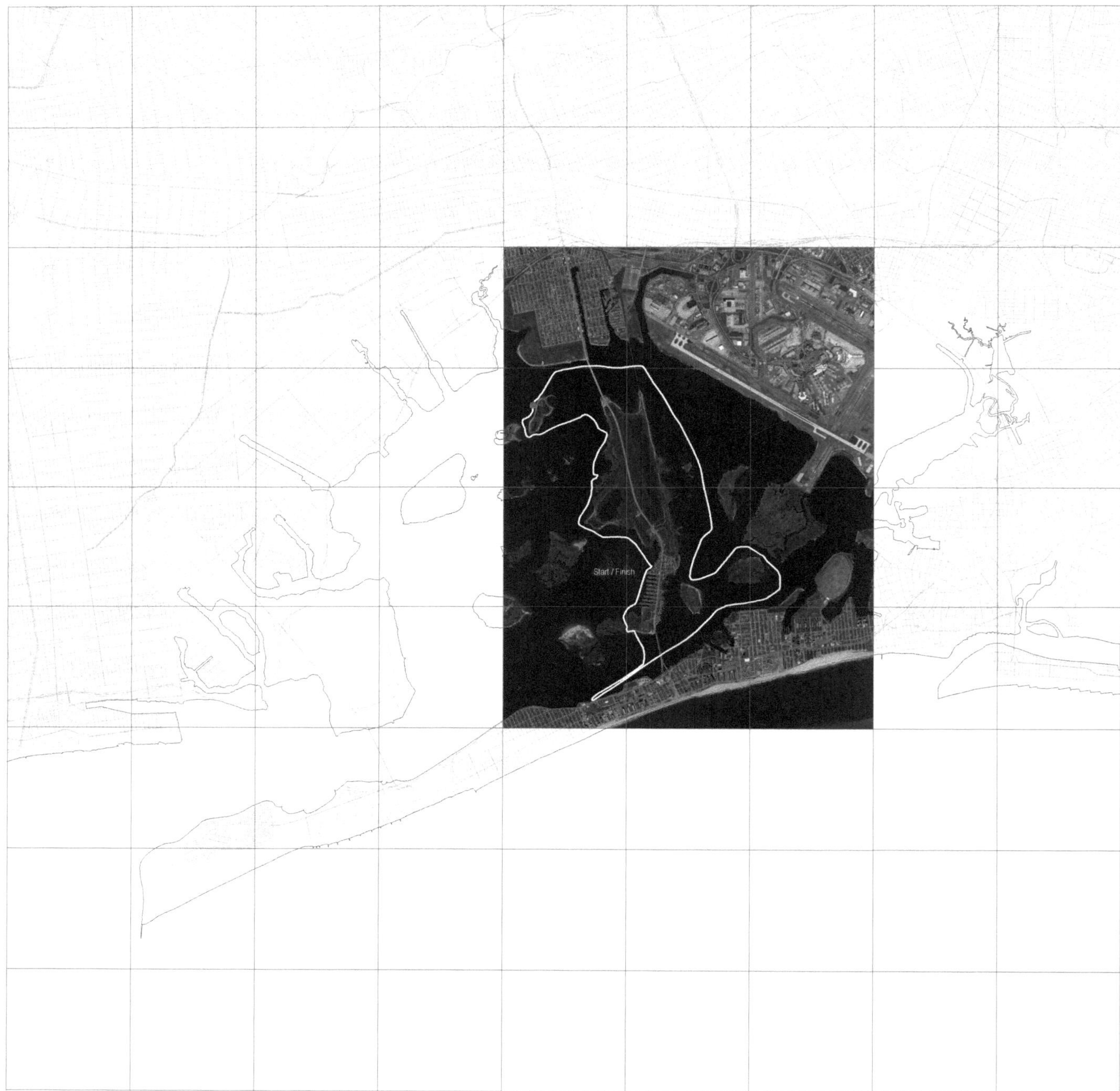

Elders Point East, Broad Creek, Subway Island, JoCo Marsh Boat Survey

Elders Point East, 2014

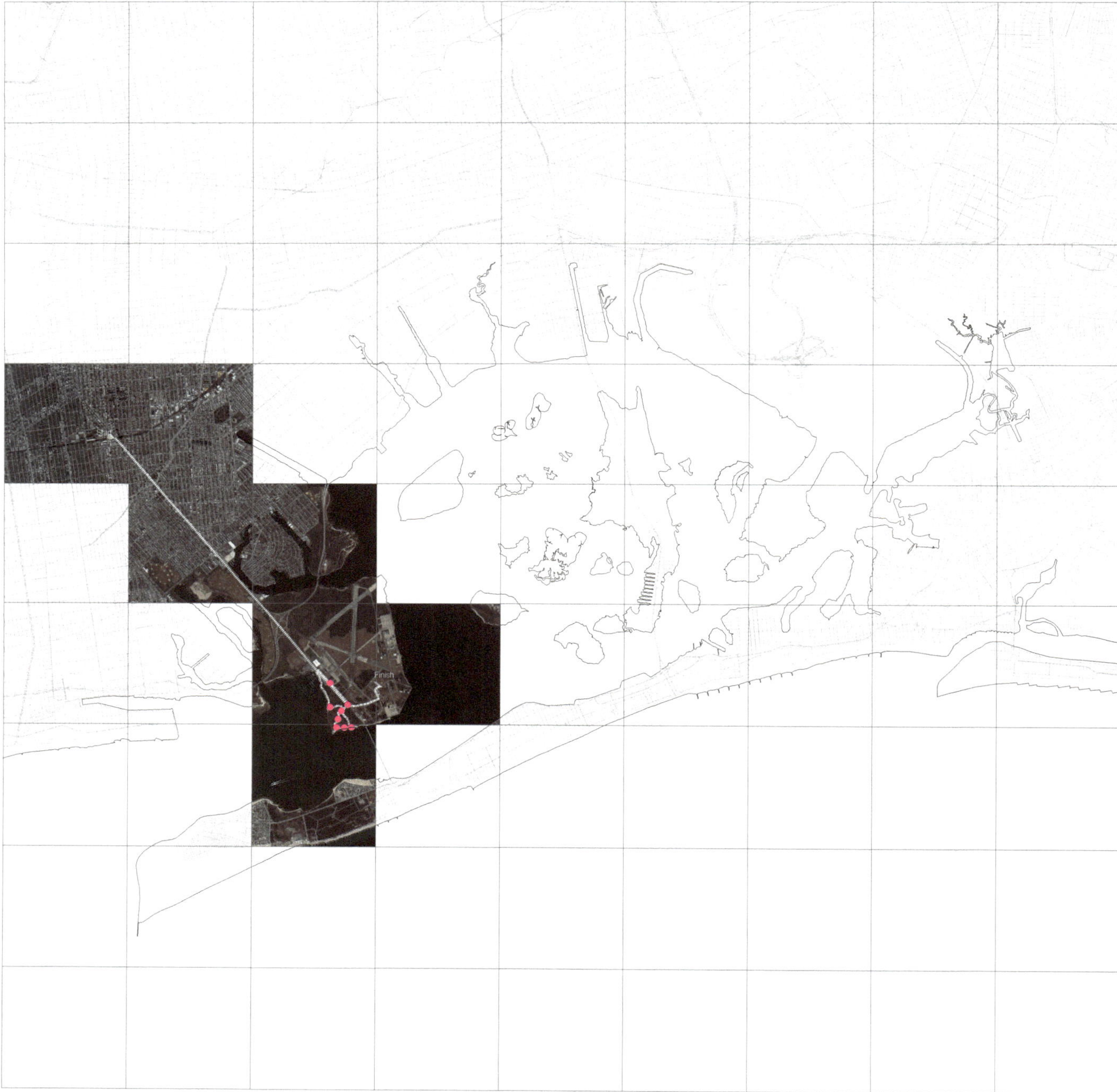

Dead Horse Bay Survey

Finish

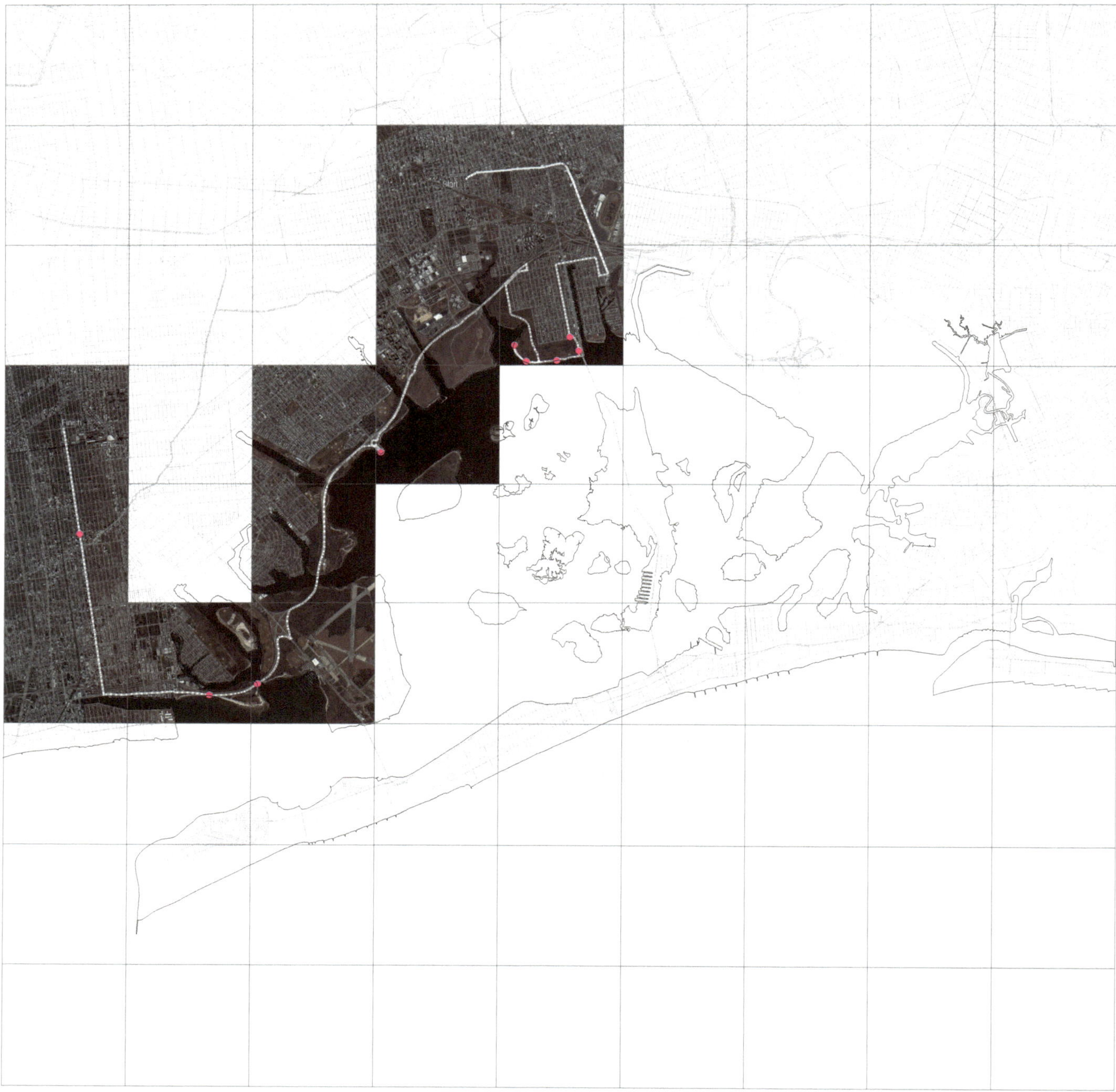

North Shore Bike Survey

Start
Finish

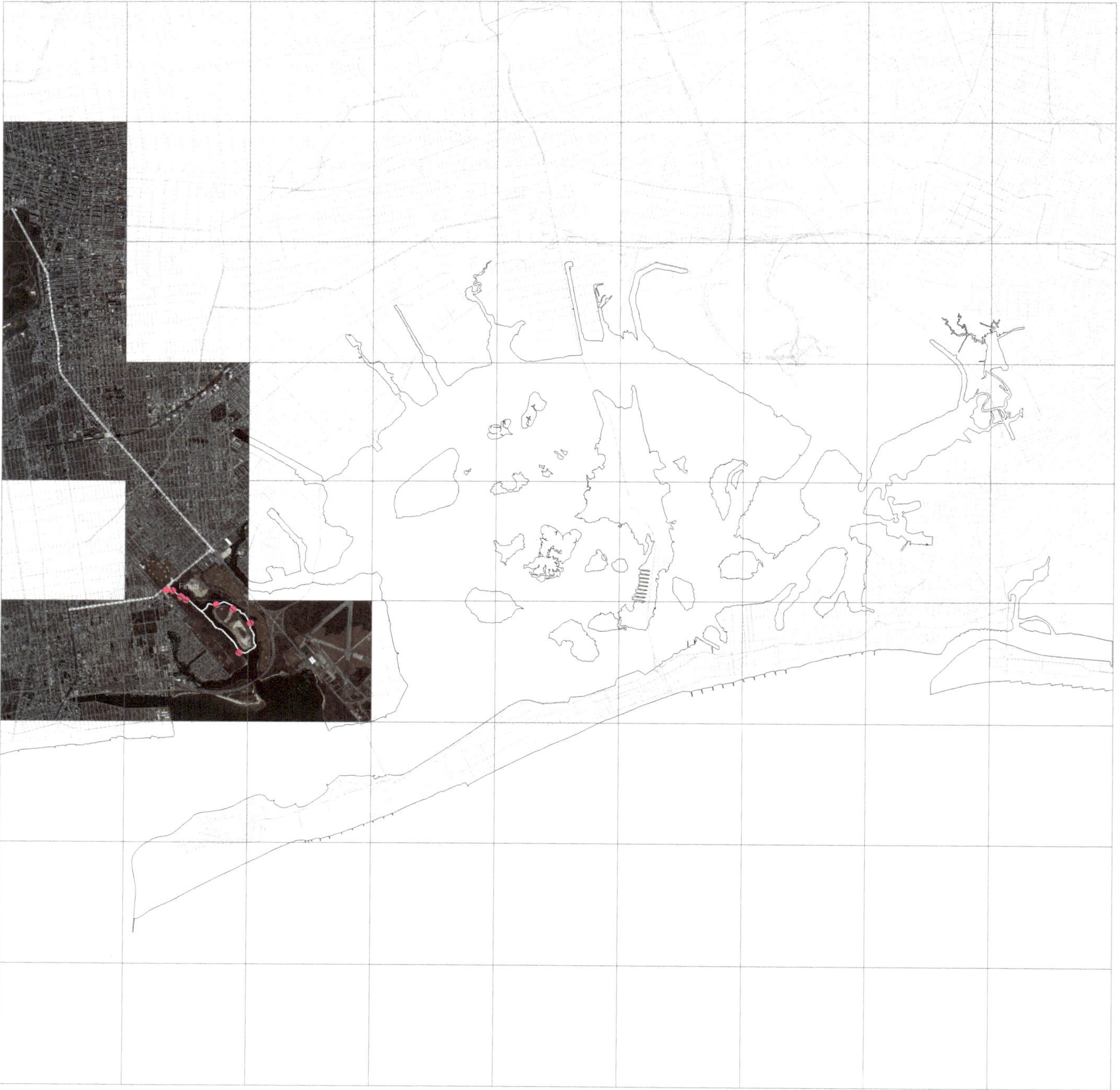

Marine Park Survey

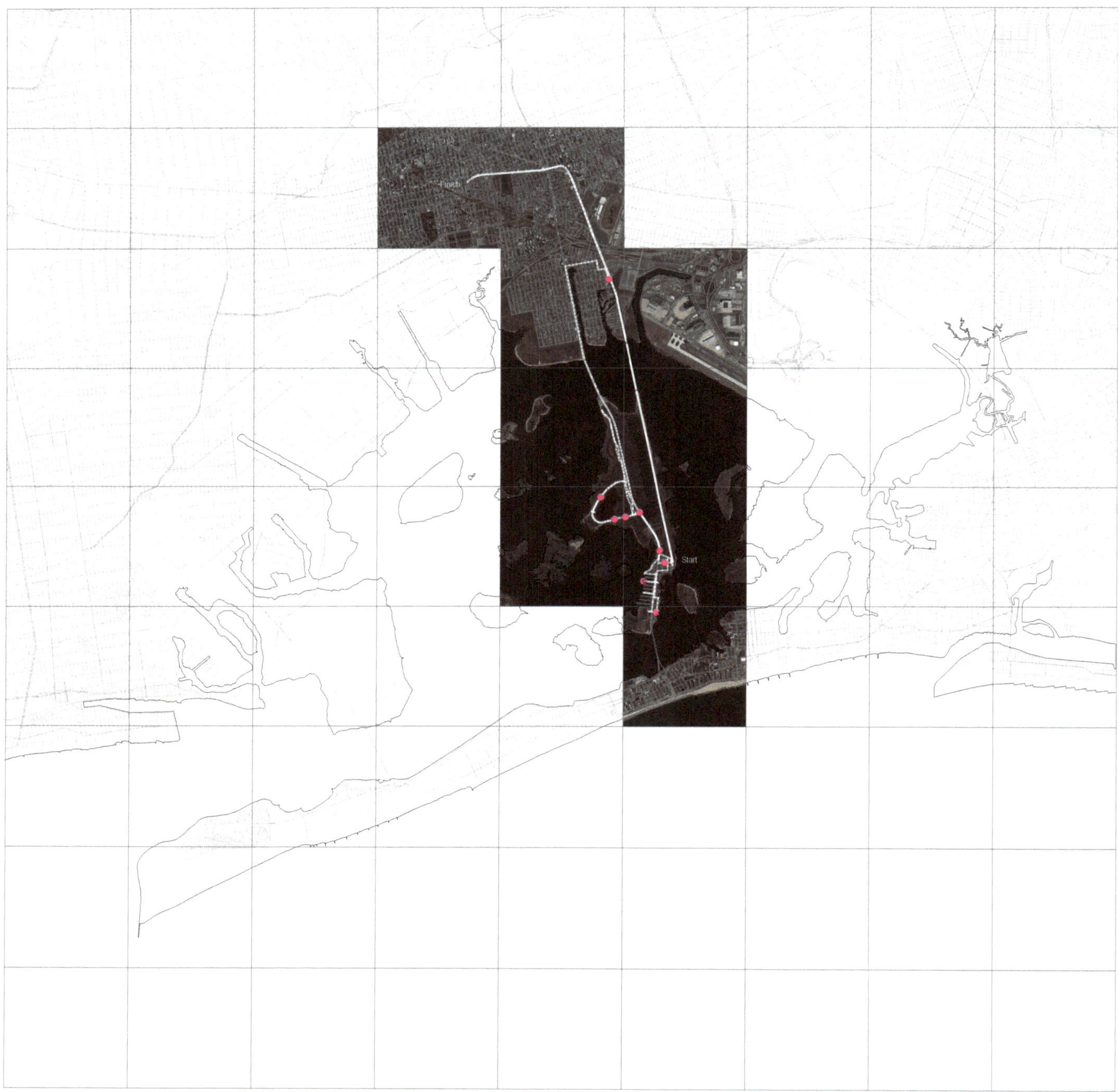

Jamaica Bay Wildlife Refuge, Broad Channel Survey

Start
CALL-A-HEAD
Lenny's
Broad Channel Station
Finish

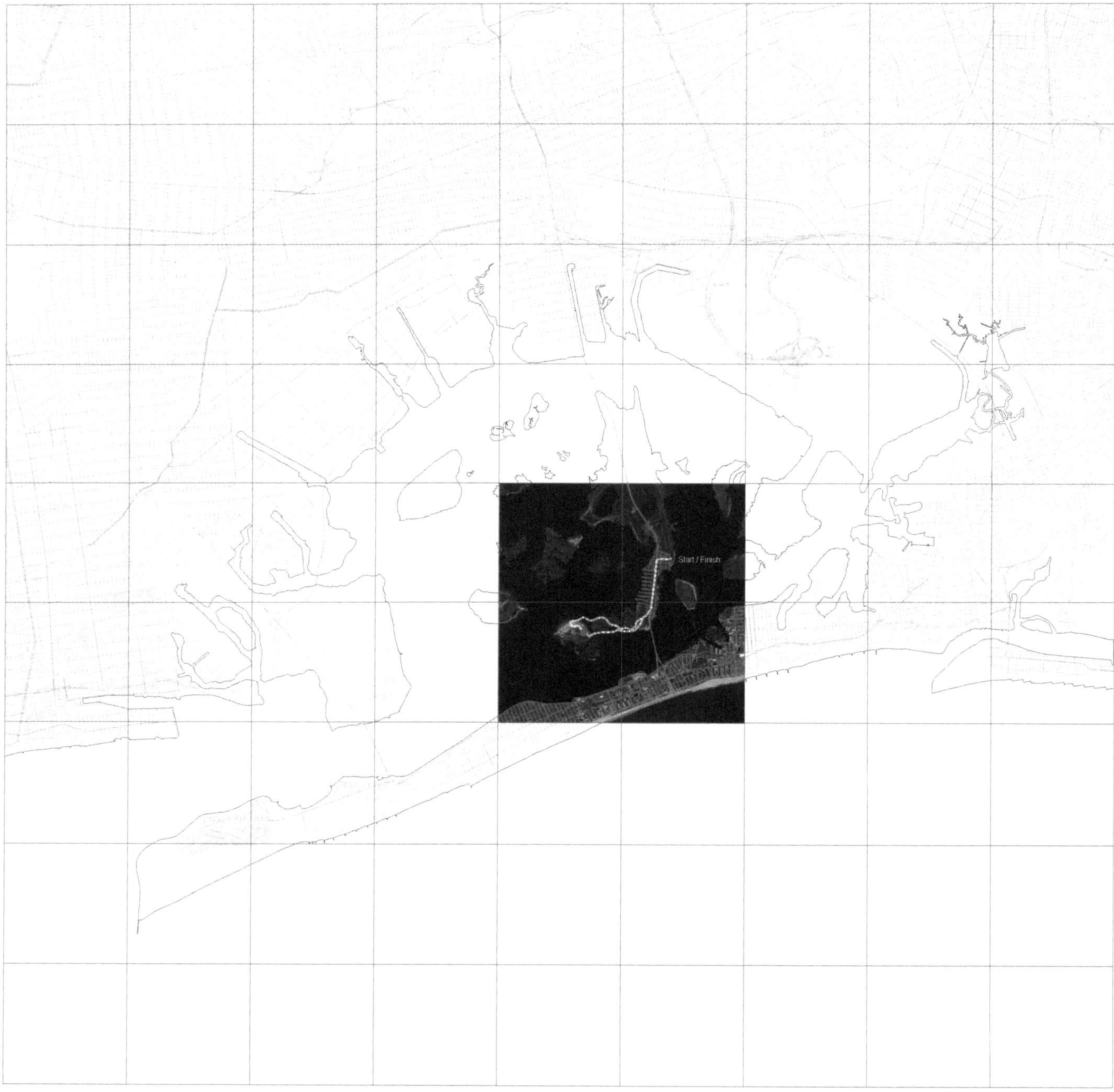

Big Egg, Little Egg Marsh Survey

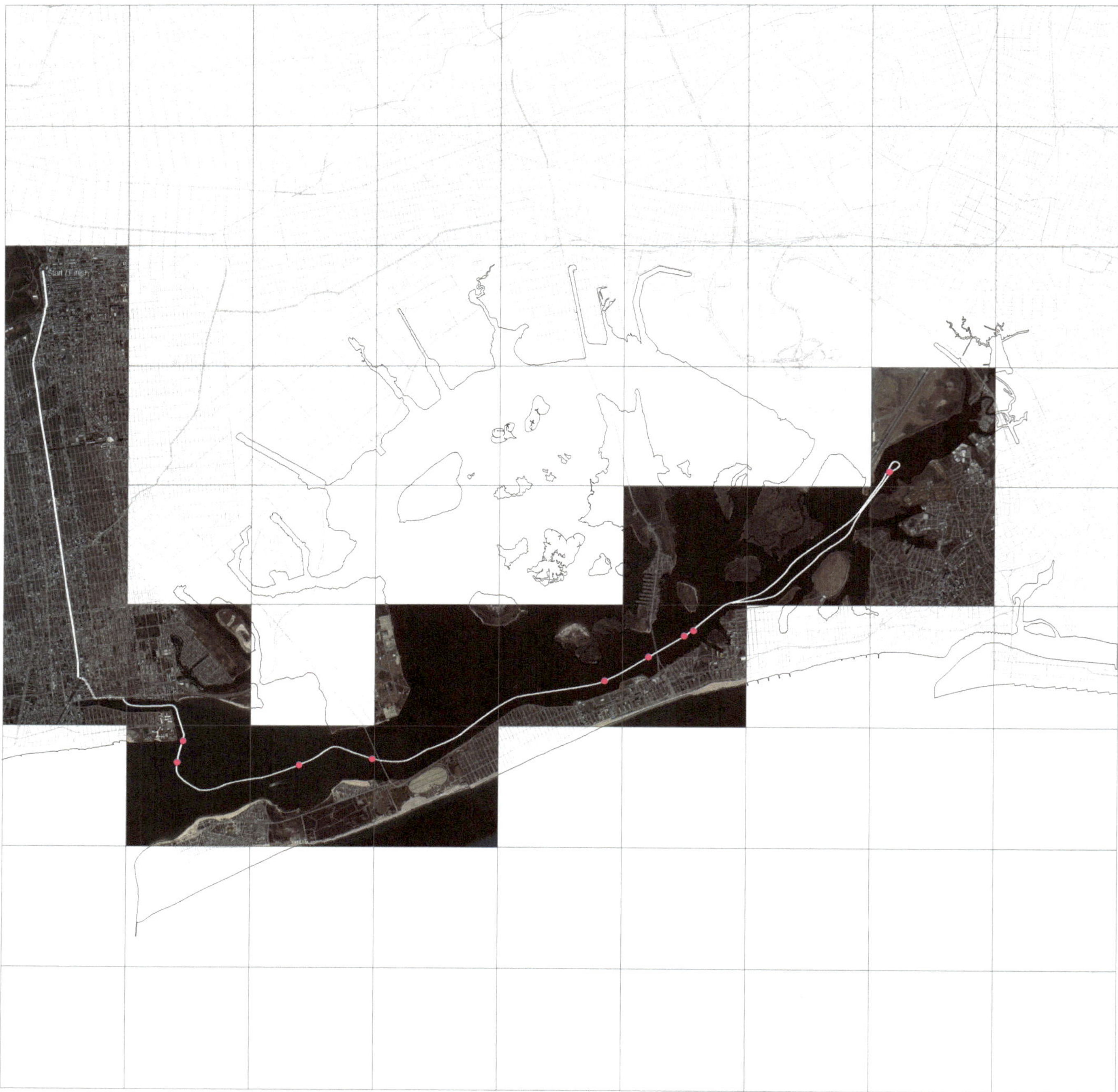

South Bay Ecology Cruise

Start
Finish

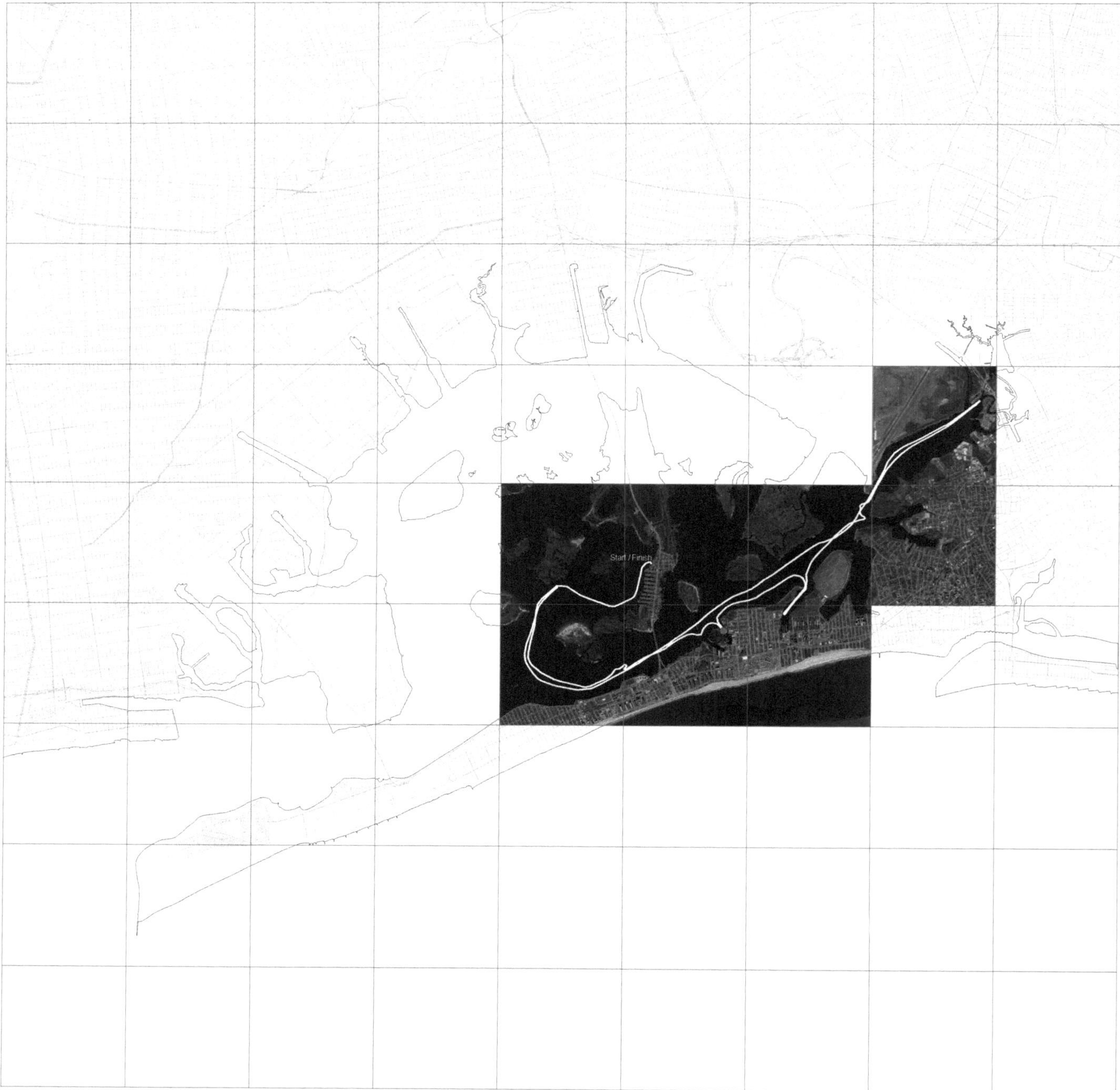

Broad Channel, Arverne, Edgemere, Bayswater, Inwood, Head of Bay Boat Survey

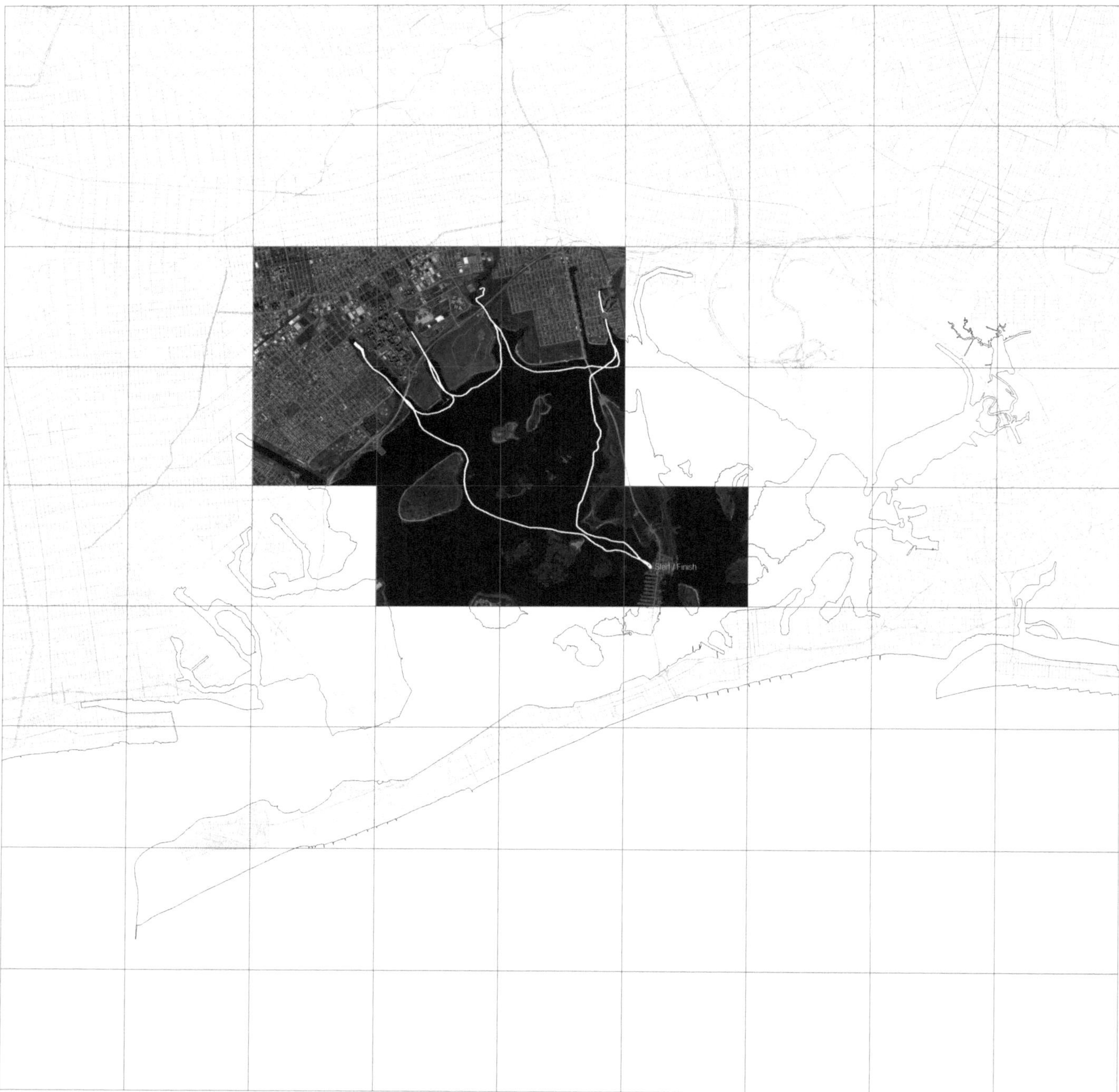

Fresh Creek, Hendrix Creek, Spring Creek, Hawtree Basin Boat Survey

www.ingramcontent.com/pod-product-compliance
Lightning Source LLC
Chambersburg PA
CBHW060826270326
41931CB00002B/82

* 9 7 8 1 9 4 2 9 0 0 1 0 8 *